To Erik, Emma, and Wyatt (aka The Committee),
for their love, inspiration, and support.
And, of course, to my friends Angus and Otis.
—H. M.

For Merial and Pat,
with love and appreciation
—L. R.

What to Expect
When Mommy's Having a Baby

Heidi Murkoff

Illustrated by Laura Rader

HarperFestival®
A Division of HarperCollinsPublishers

A Word to Parents

Congratulations—you're having another baby. You're thrilled, you're excited, you're a little nervous (will two be twice the fun, or twice the work?)—but most of all, you're wondering how you're going to explain this miraculous but extremely complex process to your older, but still very young, child.

What to Expect When Mommy's Having a Baby is a good place to begin. It isn't meant to anticipate or completely answer all of your child's questions. Rather, it's meant to give voice to some of the questions your child may have (but may not be able to clearly express) and to serve as a jumping-off point for further discussion and dialogue about how a baby is created, how it grows, and ultimately, how it comes out to join the family.

How much information is not enough? How much is too much? For that, as always, let your child be your guide. I suggest you read through the book first, so that you'll be familiar enough with the content that you can mentally add or edit as you read it to your child. The key to answering a child's questions—particularly about subjects like reproduction and the human body—is to give as much information as is requested, but no more. Keep your explanations honest, straightforward, and accurate, but geared to your child's level of comprehension. Most of all, try hard (and it will be hard!) not to appear shocked, embarrassed, or disapproving when your child broaches subjects that may be uncomfortable for you. Remember, a young child's

curiosity about everything in his or her environment is natural. By encouraging curiosity, you'll nurture a love of learning that will last a lifetime.

When is the best time to share the news about the impending birth? Most parents feel comfortable waiting until the end of the first trimester, when the pregnancy is well established. Just don't wait so long that your child hears the news from someone else. For young children, who have little concept of the passing of time, the intangible months that loom ahead can seem an eternity; it may help to tie the birth date to a familiar season or event, like spring, when the flowers come out, or your child's birthday. Be careful not to make the pregnancy the focus of family life; when your child seems to have had enough of the topic, switch gears to prevent new-baby overload.

You'll notice that I have help explaining to your child what to expect when Mommy's having a baby. Because learning should be fun, too, I've created Angus, a lovable dog who provides answers to questions about growing up. Angus serves as a best friend and confidante throughout all of the What to Expect Kids™ books. He's a "transitional object" who will hold your child's hand as he or she faces new—and sometimes challenging—experiences.

For more tips on how to prepare an older sibling for the birth of a new baby, read *What to Expect the First Year* and *What to Expect the Toddler Years*.

Wishing all the best as baby makes four (or five). . . .

Heidi

Follow me! I'll help answer your questions.

Just Ask Angus

Hello! My name is Angus. Some people call me the Answer Dog, because I like to answer all kinds of questions about growing up. It's good to ask questions because what you know, helps you grow!

So, I hear your mommy's having a baby. Congratulations! That means your family is getting bigger, and you're going to become a big brother or sister.

Did you know that there are many ways to say "having a baby"? Most people will say your mommy is pregnant. Some people will say she's expecting. They all mean the same thing—there's going to be a new baby in your house!

You and your mommy and daddy must be very excited, but I bet you have a lot of questions, too. I'm here to help—just ask me!

Are you ready to find out what to expect when your mommy's having a baby, and what you can do to help? Then let's get started! Follow me. . . .

Your friend,

Angus

P. S. I've put a little game or idea to think about on the bottom of every page. Look for my paw print, and you'll find it! Have fun!

Where is the baby?

The baby is in a special place in your mommy's belly called a uterus. Some people say womb instead of uterus. The uterus is a warm, cozy, snuggly place, the very best place for a baby to be while it's growing. Before you were born, you were in your mommy's uterus, too!

🐾 **Curl up in a little ball, and wrap yourself in a warm blanket. Now you know how it feels to be a baby inside a uterus!**

Uterus
or Womb

How did the baby get in there?

Your mommy and daddy love each other a lot, and they also love you. Together, you make a family. Being a family is so special that your mommy and daddy decided to make another baby. Making a baby is a little like putting pieces of a puzzle together. Mommies have one piece, called an ovum. Daddies have the other piece, called sperm. When a mommy and daddy want to make a baby, the daddy puts his sperm inside the mommy. The daddy's sperm fits together with the mommy's ovum. Then a baby starts growing.

Believe it or not, you were once a tiny baby growing inside your mommy's uterus. Ask to see pictures of your mommy when she was pregnant with you.

How can a baby fit inside Mommy?

A baby doesn't start out baby-size inside your mommy. In the beginning, the baby is smaller than a pea, and your mommy's belly looks the same as always. But just like you, the baby grows a little bit every day. And as it grows bigger . . . and bigger . . . and bigger . . . so does your mommy's belly!

When you were inside your mommy's uterus, you were tiny like a pea, too. Look at a pea. Now look at yourself in the mirror. See how much you've grown!

What makes the baby grow? How can I help?

The same things that make you grow, like food and rest, make the baby grow, too. Since the baby is growing inside of Mommy, she helps it grow the most. But you and Daddy can also help. You can eat healthy foods with Mommy. You can take walks together. You can take your vitamins together. You can make sure you all get plenty of rest. And since all of these things help you grow, too, you and the baby will be growing at the same time!

What's your favorite healthy food? Can you guess what mine is?

How does the baby eat?

While the baby is inside your mommy's uterus, it can't eat by itself the way you do. But it still needs food, so your mommy shares the food she eats with the baby. Inside your mommy, the food she eats changes into food that's right for the baby (babies aren't ready to eat pizza or chicken yet!). Then a special tube called the umbilical cord sends the food right to the baby's belly. When the baby is born, it will eat through its mouth, just like you. Guess what happens to the umbilical cord? It becomes a belly button!

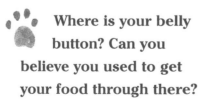

Where is your belly button? Can you believe you used to get your food through there?

Can the baby hear and see me?

The baby can hear a lot of what's going on outside your mommy's belly. It can hear your daddy reading you a story, it can hear a dog barking, it can hear the music your mommy is playing, and, best of all, it can hear you talking. That helps the baby get to know you even before it's born. The baby's eyes are open sometimes, but it can't see through the uterus. That's okay, because when the baby is born it will have lots and lots to look at—especially you!

Babies love to listen to singing. Try putting your mouth really close to your mommy's belly. Then sing your favorite song to the baby.

What does the baby do all day?

The baby does a lot of the same things that babies do after they're born. It sleeps a lot. It eats. It sucks its thumb. It wiggles around. It yawns. Sometimes it even gets the hiccups. When the baby's the size of a pea, your mommy can't feel the baby moving around. But when the baby gets bigger, she can feel it a lot. You may be able to feel the baby kicking, too, if you put your hand on your mommy's belly!

Babies like to be touched, even when they're inside their mommies. Ask your mommy if you can rub her belly gently. I bet the baby will like that!

When the baby gets bigger you can feel it move!

Why doesn't Mommy feel well sometimes?

Helping a baby grow is hard work. Sometimes your mommy may get tired, or her back may hurt a little, or she may get a stomachache. Sometimes she may not feel like eating very much. Sometimes she may feel like eating everything in sight! But that doesn't mean that she's sick—it just means that she's pregnant.

Next time your mommy doesn't feel well, see what you can do to help her feel better. Maybe you can bring her a pillow, and you can lie down together.

Why does Mommy go to the doctor so much?

These visits to the doctor are checkups for the baby. They're a lot like the checkups you have when you go to the doctor. The doctor weighs your mommy and touches and measures her belly to see how much the baby is growing. Next, the doctor listens to the baby's heartbeat. Maybe you can listen to it, too. Then it's time to answer your mommy's and daddy's questions—and yours, too!

Many times, families don't know if the baby is a boy or a girl until it's born. Even the doctor can't tell from the outside. But it's fun to guess!

When will the baby come out? How does it get out?

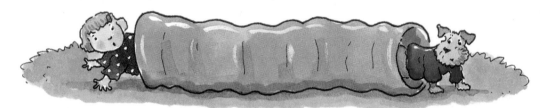

Babies need to stay in the uterus until they're big enough to be born. That usually takes about nine months, which is a pretty long time. When the baby is ready to come out, it starts moving down a tunnel called a birth canal. When it gets to the bottom of the birth canal, the baby comes out of an opening between Mommy's legs called the vagina. Your mommy and daddy will probably go to the hospital for the baby to be born, so the doctor can help. The hospital may even let you visit. And as soon as the baby is born, guess who's a big brother or sister? You are!

Ask your mommy to show you pictures of you on the day you were born. Can you believe you were ever that little?